A Discovery Biography

Martha Washington

— ◆ —

First Lady of the Land

by LaVere Anderson
illustrated by Cary

CHELSEA JUNIORS
A division of Chelsea House Publishers
New York ◆ Philadelphia

This book is for Pauline LaVere Anderson with love

The Discovery Biographies have been prepared under the
educational supervision of Mary C. Austin, Ed.D.,
Reading Specialist and Professor of Education, Case
Western Reserve University.

Cover illustration: Maria Ruotolo

First Chelsea House edition 1991

Copyright © MCMXCI by Chelsea House Publishers, a division
of Main Line Book Co. All rights reserved. Printed and bound in
the United States of America.
© MCMLXXIII by LaVere Anderson

1 3 5 7 9 8 6 4 2

ISBN 0-7910-1452-5

Contents

Chapter *1*

A Girl of Virginia

"Bessie, do squirrels like grape jelly?" ten-year-old Martha Dandridge asked.

Fat Bessie, the cook, laughed. "Miss Martha, that pet squirrel of yours will like anything you give her."

"I'll take her some jelly when it is ready and see what she does," Martha said. "Oh, this kettle is hot!"

"Be careful, child," the kindly black woman said. "Don't stand so close to the fire when you stir that jelly. What would your mama say if I let you get burned?"

Martha stepped back from the open fireplace where a kettle hung over the flames. From the big pot came the sweet smell of grapes. Martha liked to cook. On this early fall morning in 1742, Bessie was teaching her to make grape jelly.

They were in the kitchen of Chestnut Grove. This was the farm, or plantation, in Virginia where Martha had been born. The family lived in a big white house. Behind it stood small houses for the slaves. Beyond were green fields of tobacco. Martha's father, John Dandridge, raised tobacco and shipped it to England.

Virginia plantations were far apart. People met at church on Sundays, and sometimes there were big parties. But Martha had little chance to play with other girls her own age. For company she had her three brothers and two baby sisters. She and her brothers liked to race their horses over the fields. Sometimes the boys took her boating or fishing on the Pamunkey River.

Martha's days were filled with lessons. Her mother taught her to sew and to "keep house." Her father taught her to read, write, and spell. There were few schools for children then, so each family taught its own children.

Of all her lessons, Martha liked cooking the best. Now she lifted the spoon from the big pot. Purple juice fell from the spoon. "Isn't it a pretty color, Bessie!"

Bessie nodded. "It looks ready to put into jars."

Soon the jelly jars were all filled. Martha took off her apron. "Oh, dear," she said. "It's time to study my spelling. I wish spelling were as much fun as cooking."

Bessie's big laugh filled the kitchen. "You are a born cook, Miss Martha. Don't forget to take some jelly to your squirrel."

Martha had made friends with a gray squirrel that came to her bedroom window. She had named it Maybelle.

In her sunny bedroom Martha sat at the desk with her spelling book. She heard a sound at the window. There was Maybelle! Martha opened the window a little and laid a spoon of jelly on the sill.

Maybelle sniffed at it. She took a little taste. She looked at Martha and clicked her teeth.

Martha smiled. "I know. You are saying, 'Martha Dandridge, don't you *ever* have any nuts?'"

Maybelle took a last taste of jelly. Then she waved a good-bye with her tail.

Martha turned again to her spelling lesson. *Scissors.* She looked hard at the word. All those letters *s.* She counted them. Four!

"How will I ever remember where they all go?" she thought. Then she had a happier thought. "Perhaps it won't matter if I am not a good speller. When I grow up, I will never need to spell except in letters to my family. The family won't mind if a word is wrong.

"It is not as if I will ever know important people like generals and governors. I will never have to write to *them.*"

She bent over her book once more. "S-c-i-s-s-o-r-s," she began.

Chapter 2

The Governor's Ball

Five years passed quickly for busy Martha.

One bright morning she stood before the mirror in her bedroom. She smiled. The girl in the mirror smiled back.

"No!" Martha said aloud. "That was too big a grin. People will think I am silly."

She smiled again. Then she shook her head. "That one was not big enough. I will look as if I am cross. Oh, I wish I did not have to go to the governor's ball. I've never been to such a big party before. I won't know how to act."

Each year the governor of Virginia gave a great party. It was held in the governor's palace at Williamsburg, the capital city of Virginia. All the important plantation families were asked. Now that Martha was fifteen, she was invited to the party too.

Martha began to walk slowly up and down her room. Her father had said that young ladies should walk slowly in a ballroom.

"Take short steps," she told herself. "Hold your head high. *Smile.*"

Then she bent her knees to curtsy. She would have to curtsy to the governor.

Lower and lower Martha bowed. Suddenly she lost her balance and— KER-PLUNK! She fell to the floor.

Her mother came into the room. "Martha! Why are you sitting on the floor?"

Martha stood up. "I bowed too low and fell. Mama, *must* I go?"

"Of course you must go. You will be presented to the governor and his lady. Papa and I will be proud of you."

A few weeks later Martha and her parents went to Williamsburg. They stayed at an inn. There they met many friends who had also come to the party.

"I think everybody in Virginia wants to go to the governor's ball," Martha said to herself. "Everybody but me. I am sure to do something wrong."

The governor of Virginia was an Englishman sent to America by George II, king of Great Britain. Two nations —England and Scotland—were joined together in his kingdom. Virginia belonged to Great Britain and was one of her thirteen American colonies. But these colonies had been settled by Englishmen, so most colonists still thought of England as the "mother country."

On the night of the party, the governor's palace was lighted by hundreds of candles. Men and women in fine clothes filled the great ballroom. At one end of the room sat the governor and his lady.

A man called the names of people who were to be presented to them. One by one these people walked down the long room to bow before the pair. Martha's heart beat with fear as she waited.

"MISS MARTHA DANDRIDGE."

"Your turn," Martha's father said. He

gave her a little push. "Go along, my dear."

"Walk slowly," Martha told herself. "Head high. Smile."

It seemed a very long way to the end of the room. Her knees began to shake. Now she must curtsy. Suppose she fell the way she had at home?

She looked up at the governor and his lady. Her eyes grew wide with surprise. They looked so friendly!

Suddenly she was not afraid anymore. She dipped low in a beautiful curtsy.

When she stood up, she took five steps backward, as her father had told her to do. Then she turned and went back to her parents. She walked slowly, but she was so happy she felt like skipping.

"Well done, my girl," John Dandridge said. "I am proud of you."

Soon it was time for dancing to the music of violins. Many young men asked Martha to dance. They liked the pretty girl in the white dress, with her pink cheeks and shining brown hair.

One of the men was older than the others. His name was Daniel Parke Custis. He was in his thirties. Martha thought he had the kindest face she had ever seen. He asked her to dance. Then he asked her again. He brought her fruit and cake from the supper table. When the ball was over, he helped her into the Dandridge carriage.

"Well, Martha, Mr. Custis seems to like you very much," John Dandridge said as they drove back to the inn.

Martha's eyes sparkled. "Oh, papa—mama—," said the happy girl. "I am so *glad* that we came to the governor's ball!"

Chapter *3*

Mistress Custis

During the next three years, Daniel Parke Custis often visited Chestnut Grove. Pretty Martha and quiet, kindly Daniel fell in love.

"Why don't they marry?" people asked. "Martha is seventeen now. She is old enough to get married."

"Daniel's father has found fault with every girl Daniel has known," others answered. "His father is old. Daniel does not want to marry against his wishes and make him unhappy."

One day Martha and her mother

were visiting friends in Williamsburg. They met Daniel's father there.

Old Mr. Custis had never seen Martha before. Now he looked hard at this girl his son loved. He saw that she had a sweet face and a gentle manner. They talked together. Like Daniel, old Mr. Custis lost his heart to Martha.

On a summer day in 1749, Martha became Mistress Daniel Parke Custis.

Daniel was a rich man and owned many farms. He and Martha lived on a big tobacco plantation in a beautiful house called the White House. Martha ran her home well.

"I am proud of my smart wife," Daniel told her one afternoon at dinner. On Virginia plantations the main meal of the day was usually in mid-afternoon.

"Mama taught me to keep house," Martha said. "And dear old Bessie taught me to cook. But no matter how hard papa tried, he never could teach me to spell."

Daniel laughed. "I can spell, but I could never make a spice cake like this one!" He took a big bite of the cake. "After such a fine dinner, I feel like a walk. Let's hunt for wild flowers in the woods."

Sometimes Daniel's business took him to Williamsburg. Martha always went with him. There they lived in Daniel's town house, called Six Chimneys. It was not far from the governor's palace.

Life in Williamsburg was exciting for Martha. People from all the great Virginia plantations came there to visit and shop. Daniel was a good friend of the governor, and he and Martha were

invited to the governor's parties. In turn, they gave many parties. Martha wore beautiful dresses and jewels. Her carriage was one of the handsomest in Williamsburg.

One day in 1755, Daniel came home from a visit with the governor. Martha was playing with their one-year-old son, Jacky.

Daniel smiled at the baby, but his eyes were grave.

"I have bad news," he told Martha. "The war in the west is not going well. General Braddock's soldiers were beaten, and the general was killed."

"How dreadful!" Martha cried.

Great Britain and France were fighting over the rich Ohio Valley. Both said they owned it. Both had sent their soldiers to build forts and hold the land. Many Virginia men fought beside the British soldiers. General Braddock had been their commander.

"How did it happen?" Martha asked.

"The Indians were helping the French and taught them how to fight from behind trees. General Braddock was used to fighting in the open and did not understand this kind of warfare. Many of our soldiers were killed. When the general himself was wounded, a young Virginian took command. He is a colonel named George Washington.

"It is said he was very brave. Two horses were shot from under him. Yet he kept our soldiers together. If it had not been for him, more of our men would have died."

"Colonel Washington must be a fine man," Martha said.

Although the war in the west went on, it seemed far away to Martha

25

when she and Daniel returned to their quiet plantation. In time Jacky had a little sister. She was called Patsy.

Then Daniel became ill. Doctors said his heart was weak. Martha nursed him carefully and cooked special soups and puddings for him. She sat with him day and night. Still he grew worse.

On a hot afternoon in July 1757, Daniel died. He left his fortune to Martha. She was only 25, with two small children. For their sake she put on a brave smile.

She got them a puppy and baked sugar cookies for tea parties. Yet she did not feel brave. It frightened her to think of running the plantation and raising the children alone. And she missed Daniel dreadfully. She felt lost in the big house without him.

Chapter 4

Colonel George Washington

"Dinner is almost ready. Richard should be home from town soon," Mistress Chamberlayne said. She smiled at her guest.

It had been many months since Daniel died. Martha was visiting her friends, the Chamberlaynes, at their plantation near Williamsburg. Jacky, four years old, and Patsy, two, were with her. Martha would go no place without her children.

Mistress Chamberlayne looked out the

window again for her husband. Down the road came men on horseback. "Here he is. He has somebody with him— somebody in army uniform. Why, it is Colonel George Washington! How nice that Richard has brought him home."

Soon Martha was introduced to the brave soldier Daniel had told her about. He was so tall that she only came to his shoulder. For four years George Washington had been fighting in the west. Now he was commander-in-chief of the Virginia soldiers. He had come back to Williamsburg for a short time on army business.

Martha and George liked each other at once. After dinner, they sat in the parlor talking together.

She told him about her life at the White House. He told her about his plantation on the Potomac River. It

was called Mount Vernon. Martha learned that she and George were the same age. His father, like hers, had been a tobacco planter.

"When the war is over, I am going back to Mount Vernon and farm the land," he said. "I hope I will never have to leave there again."

Martha smiled. This young officer was the hero of Virginia—a great soldier and leader of men. Yet what he really wanted to be was a farmer!

It was growing dark when George got up to say good-bye.

"No, indeed, colonel," said Richard Chamberlayne when he found his guest ready to go. "Nobody leaves my house after sunset. You must stay the night."

That evening George sat on the floor and played with Jacky and Patsy. He liked the children, and they made friends with him at once. They seemed to think he was a big new toy.

Next morning George rode away. Martha had invited him to visit the White House. Soon he came for a visit. He came to see Martha every chance he got. He and Martha fell in love. George, as well as Martha, had been very lonely. He looked forward to having a family at Mount Vernon.

"We will be married as soon as I can leave the army," George told Martha. "It would be wrong for me to leave my command while the Ohio Valley is still in danger."

"I will wait," Martha said.

It was winter before the British began to win the long war. The French left the Ohio Valley. At last George felt free to marry.

How busy the White House was on

January 6, 1759! George and Martha were married there that evening.

Soft light from candles and open fires shone on the many guests all dressed in their fine clothes. The governor and his lady were present. Tables were spread with beautiful silver and dishes.

George looked very handsome in blue knee breeches and a coat lined with red silk. Martha was lovely in a yellow dress, with pearls in her hair. She wore high-heeled silk slippers, because George was so tall. Proud and happy, she stood beside him.

Jacky and Patsy watched while their mama was married to their new papa. Then there was a fine feast. Jacky enjoyed it all, but Patsy fell asleep eating her cake.

Chapter *5*

The Farmer's Wife

A coach pulled by four horses rolled down the long drive. Inside sat George and Martha Washington with the children and their nurse.

"Whoa!" the coachman called. The horses stopped.

George turned to Martha. "Welcome home, my dear," he said. "This is Mount Vernon."

Martha looked out at a square two-story house. Its white paint gleamed in the afternoon sun. New glass sparkled in the windows. Below the big lawn she could see the blue waters of the Potomac River.

"It's beautiful!" she cried.

George looked pleased. "There is a lot of work waiting to be done, though. I have been away so long that things have run down. The barns and fences need fixing. The fields must be cleared. I want to plant wheat and corn as well as tobacco. I must plant more flowers, and grass, and fruit trees too. You can see I am going to be a very busy farmer."

"The farmer's wife will help," Martha laughed.

She did help George. Her days started at sunrise. With a bunch of keys hanging from her belt, she went to unlock the storeroom. There she gave out the day's food to the cook.

Often there were guests for breakfast.

In colonial Virginia, towns were far apart, and there were few inns. Travelers spent the night at the homes of friends along the way. George ate a small breakfast—corncakes, honey, and coffee. But guests liked ham and eggs, fried apples, and fresh fish.

During the day the mistress of Mount Vernon had much to do. There were many slaves, but they needed to be trained.

Martha taught the women how to spin yarn from wool. Then she showed them how to weave the yarn into cloth. It was a rough cloth called "homespun."

She taught both men and women how to make wine, perfume, powder, and medicines. These could be ordered from England. But it took time for slow ships to cross the ocean.

George was busy too. He looked after the outside work. Mount Vernon had its own carpenters, and men to lay bricks and to shoe horses.

There were many fields to plant. There were cows to be milked and sheep to be sheared for their wool.

There was fun as well as work. Friends and family often came to visit. Everybody liked George and small, cheerful Martha. She became known as a fine hostess and a wonderful cook.

She and George went visiting too. There were hunting parties, dances, and dinners. On Sundays they drove nine miles to church.

Each fall and spring they went to Williamsburg, when the House of Burgesses met there. The burgesses were a group of Virginians who made most of the laws for the colony.

George had been elected a burgess in 1758, and he was reelected time after time. He became one of the most important members. When he spoke, the other burgesses listened carefully.

Wherever George and Martha went, they took the children. George was a loving father. He gave both the children fat ponies to ride. He gave Patsy a harpsichord, an instrument that looked much like a piano.

Pretty Patsy often sat at the harpsichord in the candlelight and played music for her papa.

Jacky was a good-natured boy, but he would not study. All he cared about was having fun. George hired a teacher, Mr. Walter MacGowan, for him. The teacher could seldom find his pupil at lesson time. Jacky was off training his dogs to hunt fox. When Jacky was

fourteen, George said he must go away to a boys' school.

It was hard for Martha to see her son go away, but she tried to be cheerful. Tears would have upset Patsy. Patsy was not well, and Martha worried about her.

As the years passed, the lovely girl grew thin and pale. Many doctors were called in, and Patsy was given all kinds of medicine. Sometimes she seemed to be better. It was at those times that Martha's laughter rang through the house. Yet soon Patsy would be ill again.

One summer day in 1773, Patsy died. She was only seventeen. Jacky, nineteen now, came home from school to stay. His mother needed him.

Jacky still didn't like books. He liked horses and dogs—and Nelly Calvert.

She was a girl he had known for a year, and she had often visited at Mount Vernon. When Christmas came, Martha and George gave her the Christmas presents they had ordered for Patsy from England. In time, Jacky and Nelly were married.

Martha did not go to the wedding. She still missed Patsy too much.

"I would cry and spoil the whole thing," she said.

Instead, she wrote a loving letter. "My dear Nelly—God took from me a daughter when June roses were blooming. He has given me another daughter about her age when winter winds are blowing, to warm my heart again."

Jacky brought pretty, merry Nelly to live at Mount Vernon. Slowly Martha learned to smile once more.

Chapter 6

War Clouds

Martha sat quietly at her dinner table while the four men talked.

George and Martha's guests were important men in the House of Burgesses. George had asked them to dinner on this spring day in 1774.

Suddenly a word rang loud in Martha's ears. *War!*

Her hand began to shake. She laid down her fork.

Why, George's friends were saying the American colonies might go to war with Great Britain!

She began to listen carefully. Soon she understood. It was the old quarrel about taxes. In 1765, the new king, George III, had tried to make the colonies pay taxes on goods from England. The colonists refused.

They told the king, "We are free men and cannot be taxed against our wishes." They told him Great Britain had no right to make any laws for them. The king said that Great Britain did have that right.

The colonists got around the tax by ordering few things from England. Women wore homespun dresses. Men did without new guns and saddles. Then the king stopped most of the taxes. Martha had hoped the trouble was over. Now—*war*?

She looked at George. There were new lines in his face.

"He is worried," she thought. "He has not told me because I have been so sad about Patsy. I must forget my own feelings and help him."

The men began to talk about trouble in Boston. Last December, some men in Massachusetts had dumped 342 big boxes of English tea into Boston harbor. They had been angry because a new tax had been put on the tea. The king punished Boston by closing its harbor to trade. No ships could get in or out. He sent British soldiers to take over the city.

Now one of the burgesses said, "Massachusetts men are ready to fight the British soldiers. Virginia must raise an army to help her."

"If King George can close a Massachusetts harbor," said another, "he will soon be closing Virginia harbors. If he can send his army to Boston, he can send it to Williamsburg. We may have to fight the British soldiers."

"You are right," a burgess said. "Massachusetts' fight is Virginia's fight too. All the colonies must stand together. Besides the tax laws, Great Britain has made other laws which we do not like. She has taken freedoms from all of us."

"Perhaps the matter can be settled peacefully," George said. "At least, we must try."

They did try. Leading men from twelve of the thirteen colonies met together in Philadelphia, Pennsylvania in 1774. This meeting was called the Continental Congress. George was one of the men sent from Virginia to the Congress. They wrote a long letter to the king. It said the colonies had a

right to govern themselves. The king paid no attention to the letter.

In all the colonies, young men began marching and drilling. In Massachusetts British soldiers were fired upon at a bridge near Concord. The British had been trying to take away the colonists' gunpowder that was hidden there. By late spring 1775, fighting had begun in other parts of New England too.

Another meeting of Congress was called. Again George traveled to Philadelphia. When he left home this time, he was wearing an army uniform. The sight made Martha shiver in the warm May air.

"Does he think it will be a long war?" she wondered. She did not worry him with her fears. The best way to help him was to send him away with a smile.

One day a letter came to Mount Vernon from George in Philadelphia. Tears rolled down Martha's cheeks as she read it.

"My dearest—," it began. It said that he had been made commander of the Continental army. He was leaving at once for Massachusetts.

He wrote: "I would find more happiness in one month with you at Mount Vernon than in fifty years of war. But the American cause is being put in my care."

Martha folded the letter and put it into her pocket. She wiped away her tears. "A general's wife does not cry!" she told herself.

General Washington! How strange that sounded to her ears. She was not surprised he had been chosen. He would make a fine general, she knew.

Virginia was the largest of the thirteen colonies, and he was Virginia's best soldier.

But General Washington would need the help of every American. How could she help? Her eyes fell on a basket that sat on a nearby table. The basket held her knitting needles and some wool. "Yes," thought Martha, "that will help."

The general's wife picked up the needles and began to knit a pair of socks for her general.

"I'll knit many pairs for him," she told herself. "His feet will never get cold no matter how deep the snow is in Massachusetts."

Chapter 7

A Nation Is Born

The British governor of Virginia was angry because the colonists had taken up arms against the king. He was especially angry at General Washington. The governor said he would send a gunboat up the Potomac River. Soldiers would burn the general's home and take Mistress Washington prisoner.

Martha was not afraid. All the same, she made sure that Mount Vernon's treasures were safe. She packed the fine silver and dishes into barrels.

"If trouble comes, we will hide the barrels in the barns," she told Lund Washington, "and then escape." Lund was George's cousin. He had come to take care of Mount Vernon while George was away at war.

At Christmas, Martha visited George in faraway Massachusetts. The general's army was in winter camp outside Boston. George wrote that he had been given a comfortable house to live in. There was little fighting in the winter months. He was homesick for her. Would she come?

"I must start at once," Martha cried. "Jacky and Nelly must come too. George needs us."

Quickly she filled her coach with good things to eat from Mount Vernon's big storeroom. She packed nuts and apples, hams, jelly, and

fruitcake. There was hardly room left in the coach for people to sit.

It was a long hard trip over rough, icy roads. But how happy George was to see her! How the lonely soldiers enjoyed the Christmas food she brought!

Martha mended George's clothes and looked after the sick. She knit socks for the soldiers. When guns boomed, she knit faster. Nobody knew how the gunfire frightened her.

In the spring George was ready to attack the British in Boston. To his surprise the British did not stand and fight. They marched onto their ships in Boston harbor and sailed away. Washington's army got ready to move on to New York.

Soon after George arrived in New York, Martha joined him there. George worried about her because he believed the British would attack there soon. Finally it was decided that she should go home.

"You must stop at Philadelphia where you will be safe," George told Martha. "Stay there until we can be sure the governor will not attack Mount Vernon."

Martha went to Philadelphia.

The Continental Congress was there too. At this meeting the Congress was working on a very great paper—the Declaration of Independence. The Declaration said the American colonies were free from Great Britain. They were a new and independent nation, the United States of America. Congress was ready to take a vote to approve the Declaration.

It was very hot in Philadelphia on

the summer afternoon Martha visited her friend Dolly Hancock. Dolly's husband, John, was president of the Congress.

The two ladies sat in Dolly's parlor, fanning themselves and talking. Outside, people were walking past the windows toward the State House where Congress met. Martha and Dolly knew a crowd was gathered there, waiting to hear about the vote.

Suddenly the bell in the State House began to ring. DING—DONG—DING—DONG— The Declaration had been appoved!

To the people outside, it was a time for celebration. But the two women in the parlor thought of their husbands. John Hancock was president of the Congress that had just passed the Declaration. George Washington led the army that fought Great Britain. If

America lost the war and the two men were caught, they would be tried for treason to the king. They would be hanged. Their wives knew it well.

But they were brave women. They tried to smile as the bell rang out.

"A new nation has been born," Dolly said.

"On July 4, 1776! It will be a day to remember," said Martha.

Four days later, July 8, Martha listened to a public reading of the Declaration in the State House yard. Then the State House bell rang again, and all the bells in the city sounded. A great crowd gathered to hear the words of the Declaration. People shot off guns and built bonfires in the streets. They cheered and cried for joy.

"The United States of America!" they shouted. What a grand name that was!

Chapter 8

Winter at Valley Forge

It was almost dark when Martha's coach drove up to Valley Forge one cold day in February 1778. Washington's soldiers were stationed there in Pennsylvania for the winter. How lonely the valley looked with the snow-covered hills closing it in.

The coach stopped before a small stone farmhouse. Martha knew this must be the command post where George lived. In the distance, she could see long rows of log huts.

A door opened. There, in the candlelight, stood the general. He hurried to her.

Once again, Martha had come to visit George, her coach filled with food from home. This would be her third winter in camp. "I do not want you with me during the summer when there is heavy fighting," George had told her. So she spent her summers at Mount Vernon. It was safe there now that the governor had gone back to England.

"George looks so much older," Martha thought as the two sat talking that night. "It is because the war has not gone well."

The Americans had won a few victories. But General Washington's small army had lost New York, and the British had captured Philadelphia.

Congress had fled to Baltimore, Maryland. Martha tried to think of some cheerful news.

"Jacky and Nelly's new baby is a dear. Everything is fine at home, and I am glad to be back with you."

"Wait until you see this camp," George said. "You may not want to stay."

"What is wrong, George?"

"Our men have no warm clothes and little food. They do not even have clean straw to sleep on. They built huts because our tents leaked. It is very cold inside those huts, and there are few blankets. Some men sit up all night by the campfires to keep from freezing. Many are sick, but we have no medicines."

His voice grew loud as the sad and angry words went on.

"Martha, there are 10,000 soldiers in this camp. At least 3,000 of them are unfit for duty because they have no shoes or coats. There is not a cow to kill for food. We have only 25 barrels of flour to feed the whole army!"

Martha's face grew grave. "What can you do?"

"Write more letters to Congress," George said. "I must beg for food and shoes and medicine. Yet I know that Congress has little money, and war costs a great deal."

"Then things could not be worse?" Martha asked.

"Of course they could!" A proud look came into George's eyes. "The men could run off and go home. They do not. They stay because they believe in freedom. They are patriots. England can never defeat such men as these!"

The next morning Martha walked down the street of log huts. She saw many soldiers huddled around their little campfires. They were thin and sick and dressed in pieces of torn uniforms. Some had wrapped rags around their bare feet. There were bloody footprints in the snow where they had walked.

Every man stood up as the general's wife passed by. "Good day to you, Lady Washington," they said. "Welcome to Valley Forge."

Love shone from Martha's eyes for these young men who stood so straight. They might look like scarecrows, but they behaved like the fine soldiers they were.

The young soldiers were to see their general's lady many times in the cold dark days to come. She went back and

forth to the camp hospital, an officer walking beside her. He carried a big pot of hot soup she had made for the sick.

Martha met the wives of other officers who had come to be with their husbands.

"Let us form a sewing group," she told them. "We can mend the soldiers' clothes and make socks for them." All the ladies were glad to help.

George's birthday came. He was 46 on February 22, 1778. Martha found some tough old hens and cooked them until they were tender for his birthday dinner.

The cruel winter dragged on. Often the soldiers drilled long hours with the snow flying in their faces. Valley Forge was only 25 miles from Philadelphia. On a clear day the cold and hungry

Americans could see the city from their camp. They knew the British soldiers there were warm and well-fed.

One day a tall, laughing French soldier came to Valley Forge. His name was Lafayette, and he was only nineteen. He was so excited by the Americans' ideas about freedom that he had come to join Washington's army.

Lafayette was an important nobleman in his own country. He knew that the American government had asked France to help the new nation in its war with England.

"I will also ask the French king to send ships and money," he promised.

It did not take the merry young officer long to win the hearts of Martha and George. George came to look upon him almost as a son. He called Lafayette "the French boy."

So the winter passed. The snow melted, and the grass grew green. On the hills pink and white dogwood flowered. The air was warm and sweet. Word came that France would help the Americans fight the British. How the soldiers cheered that news!

"We will celebrate," said the general. "We will have a parade."

The soldiers were thin. Their clothes were patched. But they polished their guns and put flowers in their hats. In the bright spring sunshine they marched, heads high. The camp band played every tune it knew, and then started all over again.

To Martha it was a wonderful sight. She could tell by George's face that he was proud and happy too. The terrible winter of Valley Forge was past.

With France's help, the war would be

won. George was right, she realized. England could never defeat such men as these!

In time the Americans did win the war, but it took five more years. Martha spent part of every winter with George, wherever he was. She sewed, knit, and cooked for the sick. She was always helpful and cheerful, and nobody ever heard her complain. Even when Jacky joined the army and died of camp fever, Martha did not let anyone see her tears. The soldiers all liked the general's lady. They said she did her part to help win the war.

Chapter 9

Home to Mount Vernon

It was Christmas Eve, 1783, at Mount Vernon.

The sweet smell of bayberry candles filled the rooms. Evergreens hung from the walls. In the kitchen the cook was busy making a Christmas feast. Everybody was happy, and Martha was the happiest of all. General Washington had just come home from the war!

There were children to welcome him.

"Merry Christmas, grandpapa!" cried little Nelly.

"Mer-ry Criss-mus!" shouted her small brother George.

George lifted them up and hugged them. Martha watched with a loving smile.

They were her grandchildren. Jacky and Nelly had had four children. After Jacky died, Nelly married again and went to live with her new husband. The two youngest children stayed behind. Martha and George adopted them. Dark-haired little Nelly was four now. Her brother George was almost two. He had been named for George Washington. People called him "Little Washington" and sometimes "Mr. Tub."

George was glad to be home, the war over and won. Soon after Christmas he began to make plans for Mount Vernon.

"We will raise more turkeys, geese, pigs, sheep, cows, horses, and mules," he told Martha. "That means we must build another barn. We must add more rooms to the house, too, and plant more trees and flowers. We will make Mount Vernon one of the finest plantations in Virginia."

"I can see we will be busy," Martha laughed.

One summer day George got a present. His friend Lafayette sent him seven giant hunting dogs from France. They were very fierce. Everyone was afraid of them except George and Mr. Tub. By now the little boy was four. He wanted to ride horses like his grandpapa, but a horse was too big for him. One morning a stableboy ran to the house to find Martha and George.

"Mr. Tub is with Vulcan!" cried the frightened boy. "That mean old dog got out of his pen. He'll *bite* Mr. Tub!"

Martha's face turned white. She and

George ran to the stable. Suddenly they stopped. George began to laugh.

There was Vulcan, walking slowly around the yard. On his broad back sat Mr. Tub. Vulcan was just the right size for a little boy to ride, and Vulcan liked playing horse!

Vulcan was put back into his pen. Mr. Tub was scolded.

"No more dog-riding!" Martha told him while George still laughed.

Mount Vernon was always full of guests. Some of them stayed for weeks. Martha and George seldom sat down to a meal alone. George told a friend, "I have 101 cows, but I still have to buy butter to feed all our guests."

Among the guests were men from Congress. They were worried about the new nation. Each state made its own laws and had its own leaders. The men said that Congress did not have enough power to govern the country.

"We need a better government," they said. "We need a Congress that has more power, and there should be one man to lead all the states."

Martha grew fearful. Would they ask George to be the leader? She hoped not. She knew he did not want to leave Mount Vernon again.

A meeting of men from all the states was held in Philadelphia. George was there. The men planned a new strong government. They wrote down what powers it should have. They called their plan the Constitution. They sent copies to the states for adoption. Then Congress met again to elect a president. He must be somebody all the people trusted. They elected George Washington.

Chapter *10*

The First Lady

Martha stood at the door of the crowded room. It was the parlor of the president's mansion in New York City, the nation's first capital. "So many people waiting to meet us!" she thought.

She was giving her first party as the wife of the president. She wanted to make George proud. She wasn't sure she could. "How does a president's wife act?" she wondered. There was nobody to ask. Suddenly Martha remembered another important party a long time

ago. "Walk slowly," somebody had said. "Head high. Smile."

"Of course!" thought Martha. "Papa!"

Slowly the president's wife walked through the door, head high, smiling.

It was a fine party. George moved among the guests, greeting each one. Martha sat on a sofa and talked to many people. They all liked friendly Mistress Washington.

So Martha's life as the First Lady began that spring of 1789. The nation had never had a First Lady before. She had to make her own rules. It was the same for George. He was the first president of the United States.

George knew that as president he would set the example for presidents to come. This worried him. How could he be sure that he would act wisely and set the right example?

"I am just a farmer and a soldier," he told Martha.

"You are a *president*!" she said.

Martha was glad when the capital was moved from New York to Philadelphia. She felt more at home there. She went to balls, dinners, and theater parties. She took the children on shopping trips. She wrote long letters to friends. Sometimes she had to stop and think about a word. Then she smiled and said to herself:

"Martha Dandridge, you should have studied harder on your spelling. Maybe you aren't writing to generals and governors, but you *are* writing to their wives!"

Martha did not care for public life. She counted the days until George's four years as president would be over.

George had been a good president,

but the new nation was still weak. It still needed a strong man like George to lead it. He was elected for another four-year term.

Martha tried hard to hide her disappointment. Head high, smiling, she went to the balls and dinners. She did not forget she was the president's wife. She wrote a friend:

"The dearest wish of my heart is to go back to Mount Vernon. Yet I cannot blame George for obeying the voice of his country."

Slowly the years passed. They were hard ones for George. England and France were at war again. Spain was making trouble for the United States. Some of the states quarreled among themselves. There was little money to run the government. But somehow George kept the nation on its feet.

One morning cannon fire awakened Martha. It sounded like Valley Forge again. She jumped out of bed.

"What is happening?" she cried.

Martha soon found out. It was February 22, 1796. Americans were celebrating George Washington's 64th birthday. Church bells rang, and all day people came to the president's house to wish him well. Martha had punch and cake ready for everyone. In the evening there was a big party.

At last the four years were over. George was asked to serve a third term. "No," he said. "It is time for another man." John Adams, the vice-president, was elected president.

Martha and George returned to Mount Vernon. Nelly went with them, but her brother stayed at school.

Mount Vernon was beautiful as they

drove toward it. The fresh green grass and first flowers of spring made home look like a fairyland to Martha.

"We'll never leave again," she said.

They had three happy years doing the things they loved best. Then on a winter day in 1799, George died after a short illness. Martha lived on at Mount Vernon. Friends and family came for long visits. They always found her cheerful. She missed George terribly, but she remembered what he had often said: "It is better to go laughing than crying through life."

On May 22, 1802, Martha died. She was almost 70 years old.

Americans honor George Washington as "The Father of His Country." Martha is honored too. She was a great and good lady, the first "First Lady of the Land."